Artificial Intelligence: How It Will Change Your Life Today

RIZO BOTIROV

Table of Contents

Section 1: Introduction to Artificial Intelligence_____3

Section 2: Core Concepts of AI_____12

Section 3: Artificial Intelligence in Everyday Life____20

Section 4: AI in Business_____31

Section 5: Ethics and Risks of AI_____42

Section 6: AI and the Future of Technology_____52

Section 7: How to Get Started with AI_____62

Section 8: Machine Learning in Detail_____69

Section 9: Deep Learning and Neural Networks_____76

Section 10: AI for Entrepreneurs and Startups_____87

Section 11: Implementing AI in Companies_____97

Section 12: The Future of Artificial Intelligence and Its Role in Society_____106

Section 1: Introduction to Artificial Intelligence

What is Artificial Intelligence?

Artificial Intelligence (AI) is a field of computer science that focuses on creating machines capable of performing tasks that require human-like intelligence. These tasks include decision-making, problem-solving, language understanding, and perception. The essence of AI lies in its ability to process vast amounts of data and draw meaningful insights, often in real-time. AI-powered systems are designed to mimic human cognition, enabling machines to "learn" from experience, adapt to new inputs, and carry out functions with minimal human intervention.

AI is often confused with automation, but they are fundamentally different. Automation refers to machines carrying out predefined instructions, while AI involves dynamic learning and adaptability. Modern AI has been incorporated into various industries, ranging from healthcare to finance, changing the way businesses and people interact with technology.

The History of AI Development

The concept of artificial intelligence has roots in ancient history, with the idea of intelligent machines appearing in myths and legends. However, the modern pursuit of AI began in the mid-20th century. In 1956, at the Dartmouth Conference, the term "Artificial Intelligence" was officially coined by John McCarthy, and it became a recognized field of research.

The 1960s and 1970s saw significant advancements, particularly in rule-based systems, known as expert systems, which were designed to replicate human decision-making. Although these systems were impressive, they lacked true learning abilities. The 1980s and 1990s brought machine learning into the spotlight, where computers began learning from data rather than relying solely on static rules.

The real leap occurred in the 21st century with the explosion of big data and the development of more powerful computational hardware. Deep learning, a subset of machine learning, began to revolutionize industries, leading to breakthroughs in image recognition, natural language processing, and even autonomous driving. AI has since become one of the most transformative technologies in history, paving the way for innovations that were once considered science fiction.

Types of Artificial Intelligence

AI can be broadly categorized into three types, each with distinct characteristics and capabilities:

1. **Narrow AI (Weak AI):** Narrow AI is designed for specific tasks. It excels in single-use cases like language translation, facial recognition, or voice assistance but lacks general intelligence. Examples include Siri, Alexa, and Google Translate.

2. **General AI (Strong AI):** General AI is theoretical at this stage. It refers to machines that can perform

any intellectual task a human can, adapting to new environments and situations with human-like reasoning and decision-making.

3. **Superintelligent AI:** This is a speculative form of AI that surpasses human intelligence in all fields, including creativity and problem-solving. While we are far from this stage, it remains a topic of extensive debate and ethical concern.

Why is AI Important Today?

AI's importance today stems from its ability to process vast quantities of data at speeds and with precision that surpass human capabilities. In business, AI is revolutionizing sectors like finance, healthcare, and manufacturing by enhancing decision-making and increasing efficiency. In healthcare, AI algorithms analyze medical data, providing insights that help diagnose diseases faster and more accurately. AI-driven automation in factories optimizes production, reduces waste, and improves quality control.

AI also plays a pivotal role in addressing global challenges such as climate change, by helping scientists model environmental changes and predict outcomes with greater accuracy. Its presence in daily life—through personal assistants, smart homes, and recommendation systems—demonstrates how seamlessly it integrates with our routines, making tasks easier and improving our overall quality of life.

Common Myths about AI

There are several misconceptions about AI, which often arise from misunderstandings or popular media portrayals. Let's address some of the most common myths:

1. **Myth 1: AI Will Soon Replace All Human Jobs**
   While AI is automating certain jobs, especially repetitive or dangerous ones, it is also creating new

industries and opportunities. Human creativity, emotional intelligence, and problem-solving abilities remain irreplaceable.

2. **Myth 2: AI Will Become Sentient and Take Over the World**
   Although this is a popular theme in movies, current AI technology is far from achieving consciousness. AI operates within the parameters defined by humans, and its decisions are based on pre-existing data.

3. **Myth 3: AI is Only for Large Corporations**
   AI tools have become more accessible, and small businesses are

leveraging AI for everything from customer service chatbots to marketing analytics, leveling the playing field in many industries.

4. **Myth 4: AI Can Solve Every Problem**

   AI is not a magic bullet. It requires quality data, appropriate training, and clear goals. Misuse of AI can lead to biased outcomes or even failure if not properly implemented.

Section 2: Core Concepts of AI

Machine Learning: The Foundation of AI

Machine learning (ML) is a subset of AI that gives computers the ability to learn without being explicitly programmed. Unlike traditional programming, where specific rules are written by developers, ML allows computers to identify patterns in data and make decisions based on those patterns.

ML is often categorized into three types:

1. **Supervised Learning:** The model is trained on labeled data, meaning the input comes with the correct output. The system uses this data to make predictions or classifications.

2. **Unsupervised Learning:** The model works with unlabeled data, identifying patterns or relationships without any predefined categories. This approach is often used for clustering or anomaly detection.
3. **Reinforcement Learning:** The system learns by interacting with its environment and receiving feedback in the form of rewards or penalties. This technique is popular in game development and robotics.

Algorithms and Their Role in AI

Algorithms are at the core of AI. An algorithm is a set of instructions or rules followed by a machine to solve a problem or perform a task. In AI, algorithms range from simple decision trees to more complex neural networks.

Popular algorithms include:

- **Linear Regression:** Used for predicting a value based on the relationship between variables.
- **Decision Trees:** Used for classification and regression, decision trees break data down into simpler structures.
- **Neural Networks:** Modeled after the human brain, neural networks are

designed to recognize patterns in complex data.

Neural Networks and Deep Learning

Neural networks are a crucial element of deep learning, which is a subset of machine learning. Inspired by the human brain, neural networks consist of layers of nodes, called neurons, that process data. Each neuron takes an input, processes it, and passes it on to the next layer.

Deep learning involves multiple layers of these neurons, allowing the model to understand and learn from vast amounts of data. This technology has led to breakthroughs in image recognition, speech processing, and even self-driving cars.

Key Programming Languages for AI

Several programming languages are widely used in AI development:

- **Python:** The most popular language for AI due to its simplicity and the vast availability of libraries like TensorFlow and PyTorch.
- **R:** Known for its statistical analysis capabilities, R is often used in machine learning projects.
- **Java:** Used in large-scale AI applications, particularly in enterprise settings.

- **C++:** Known for its speed, C++ is used in performance-critical AI applications.

Major AI Platforms and Tools

AI development is supported by a wide range of tools and platforms. Some of the most prominent include:

- **TensorFlow:** An open-source library developed by Google for deep learning applications.
- **PyTorch:** A popular machine learning framework, known for its flexibility and ease of use.

- **Microsoft Azure AI:** A cloud-based AI platform that provides tools for building and deploying AI models.
- **Google Cloud AI:** A suite of AI and machine learning tools provided by Google Cloud, allowing developers to build and scale AI solutions.

These core concepts of AI form the foundation for more advanced applications and innovations that are driving the future of technology.

Section 3: Artificial Intelligence in Everyday Life

How AI is Already Changing Our Lives

Artificial Intelligence has become an integral part of our daily lives, often without us even realizing it. From our smartphones to online shopping, AI is embedded in numerous tools and services we use regularly. The transformative power of AI is visible in how it makes everyday tasks faster, smarter, and more convenient.

For instance, when you scroll through social media feeds, AI algorithms analyze your behavior and recommend content that aligns with your interests. When you shop online, AI is behind personalized recommendations, helping businesses suggest products that match your preferences. Even in entertainment, platforms like Netflix and Spotify use AI to recommend movies and music based on your viewing and listening habits.

AI-powered solutions are also making waves in transportation with self-driving cars, ride-sharing services, and traffic management systems. These innovations are aimed at reducing human error, optimizing routes, and making travel more efficient. The impact of AI is evident in industries like finance, where automated trading systems, fraud detection algorithms, and customer service chatbots are transforming operations. AI is deeply integrated into the fabric of modern society, revolutionizing how we interact with technology.

Voice Assistants (Siri, Alexa, Google Assistant)

Voice assistants, such as Siri, Alexa, and Google Assistant, have brought AI into our homes, offices, and mobile devices, creating a new way of interacting with technology. These intelligent virtual assistants use natural language processing

(NLP) to understand spoken commands and perform a wide range of tasks, from setting reminders to controlling smart home devices.

One of the primary functions of voice assistants is to provide quick access to information. Whether you need weather updates, calendar notifications, or directions, voice assistants respond in real-time. They have also become central hubs for managing smart home devices, allowing users to control lights, thermostats, security systems, and even appliances with simple voice commands.

Siri, Alexa, and Google Assistant are continuously learning and evolving. Over time, they become more personalized, adapting to your speech patterns, preferences, and routines. The growing use of these AI-driven assistants signifies the shift toward more hands-free, efficient ways of interacting with technology, simplifying everyday tasks and enhancing convenience.

Smart Homes and Devices

The rise of smart homes and devices is one of the most significant ways AI is reshaping our living environments. AI-powered systems now allow homes to be interconnected, with devices communicating with each other to provide a seamless living experience. From smart thermostats that learn your preferred temperature settings to smart refrigerators that alert you when you're low on groceries, AI-driven devices are making homes more efficient and comfortable.

One of the key advantages of smart homes is energy efficiency. Smart thermostats like Nest and Ecobee adjust heating and cooling based on your daily habits, helping reduce energy consumption and lower utility bills. Smart lighting systems, such as Philips Hue, can be programmed to turn off when no one is in the room or change brightness based on natural light levels.

AI also enhances security through smart cameras, doorbells, and alarm systems. These devices can recognize faces, send real-time alerts to homeowners, and even differentiate between potential threats and harmless activity. With AI, the concept of home automation has evolved beyond convenience to improve sustainability, security, and personalized living.

AI in Medicine and Healthcare

AI is revolutionizing medicine and healthcare, leading to more precise diagnoses, personalized treatment plans, and even predictive health monitoring. Medical professionals now have access to AI tools that analyze vast datasets, identify patterns, and offer insights that were previously unattainable.

One of the most significant advancements in healthcare AI is in medical imaging. AI algorithms can scan and interpret images like X-rays, MRIs, and CT scans faster and more accurately than human doctors in some cases, identifying conditions such as cancer, fractures, and tumors. AI-powered diagnostic tools assist physicians in detecting diseases at earlier stages, improving patient outcomes.

In healthcare management, AI-driven systems help optimize hospital operations, predict patient admission rates, and streamline administrative tasks. AI-powered chatbots and virtual health assistants also assist patients by answering medical questions, scheduling appointments, and providing medication reminders.

Personalized medicine is another area where AI is making strides. AI analyzes a patient's genetic data to recommend personalized treatment plans, leading to more effective care. AI's potential in healthcare extends to drug discovery, where machine learning models accelerate the identification of potential drug candidates, reducing the time and cost involved in bringing new drugs to market.

AI in Education and Learning

Artificial Intelligence is transforming education, making learning more personalized, accessible, and efficient. AI-powered tools are reshaping how students learn and how educators teach, paving the way for adaptive learning platforms, virtual classrooms, and personalized education plans.

One of the most prominent applications of AI in education is adaptive learning platforms that tailor content to the individual needs of students. These systems, like DreamBox and Knewton, analyze a student's strengths, weaknesses, and learning pace to adjust the difficulty of lessons and provide personalized recommendations. As a result, students receive a more tailored learning experience, enhancing understanding and retention of information.

AI also plays a crucial role in grading and assessment. Automated grading systems can evaluate multiple-choice tests and even essays, saving educators valuable time. These systems can provide detailed feedback on student performance, allowing teachers to identify areas where students may need additional support.

Additionally, AI-driven virtual tutors are becoming increasingly popular. These tutors assist students in areas like math, science, and language learning by providing interactive lessons and personalized feedback. AI also enables more inclusive learning experiences, offering tools for students with disabilities, such as text-to-speech software and real-time translations.

Section 4: AI in Business

How AI is Transforming Business Models

Artificial Intelligence is reshaping business models across industries by introducing automation, improving decision-making, and enhancing customer experiences. AI-driven technologies are enabling businesses to operate more efficiently, innovate faster, and gain a competitive edge. From small startups to large corporations, AI is now a crucial component in driving growth and success.

One of the most transformative aspects of AI in business is automation. Routine tasks such as data entry, customer support, and even supply chain management can now be handled by AI-powered systems. These systems operate around the clock, increasing productivity while reducing human error. Robotic Process Automation (RPA), for example, enables companies to automate repetitive tasks, freeing up employees to focus on higher-value work.

AI is also enhancing decision-making through advanced data analytics. By analyzing vast datasets, AI can provide businesses with actionable insights that help in forecasting, trend analysis, and strategic planning. Predictive analytics models enable companies to anticipate market shifts, customer behavior, and supply chain disruptions, helping them make informed decisions that drive long-term success.

AI in Marketing and Advertising

AI has revolutionized marketing and advertising by enabling businesses to reach their target audiences more effectively and deliver personalized experiences. From targeted ads to automated customer segmentation, AI has transformed how companies engage with consumers and manage marketing campaigns.

AI-powered tools analyze consumer data, such as online behavior, purchasing patterns, and demographics, to create personalized marketing campaigns. Algorithms identify which products a customer is most likely to buy, enabling companies to send personalized recommendations and promotions. This targeted approach increases conversion rates and enhances customer satisfaction.

Programmatic advertising is another area where AI has made significant strides. Through AI, companies can automate the buying and selling of digital ads, ensuring that ads are shown to the right people at the right time. AI-driven platforms such as

Google Ads and Facebook Ads use machine learning to continuously optimize ad performance, ensuring maximum ROI for marketing spend.

AI in Analytics and Big Data

Data is the lifeblood of AI, and businesses are leveraging AI to analyze massive datasets, uncover trends, and extract actionable insights. AI-powered analytics tools provide real-time data processing and visualization, enabling businesses to make data-driven decisions quickly and accurately.

In the era of big data, AI helps businesses identify patterns and correlations that would otherwise be impossible to detect. AI-driven analytics platforms such as Tableau, Power BI, and Qlik allow businesses to analyze structured and unstructured data, transforming raw information into meaningful insights. These tools help companies in areas like demand forecasting, customer behavior analysis, and financial planning.

AI's role in big data analytics extends beyond traditional methods. Through natural language processing, AI can analyze unstructured data like customer reviews, social media posts, and emails, providing businesses with a comprehensive view of customer sentiment. This level of analysis helps businesses understand market trends and customer preferences, allowing for more targeted and effective strategies.

How Companies are Implementing AI

Companies across industries are adopting AI to streamline operations, enhance customer experiences, and drive innovation. From retail to finance, AI is becoming a strategic priority for businesses looking to stay competitive in a rapidly evolving market.

In the retail industry, companies like Amazon are using AI to optimize supply chain management, improve product recommendations, and create seamless shopping experiences. AI-powered chatbots and virtual assistants are becoming standard tools for enhancing customer service, providing real-time assistance to consumers 24/7.

In the financial sector, AI is transforming everything from fraud detection to investment management. Banks and financial institutions use AI algorithms to detect suspicious transactions, manage risk, and automate trading processes. Robo-advisors, powered by AI, offer personalized investment recommendations based on a customer's financial goals and risk tolerance.

Case Studies of AI-Driven Businesses

1. **Amazon:** Amazon is a pioneer in using AI to improve its e-commerce platform. From personalized product recommendations to AI-powered supply chain management, the company relies on AI to optimize operations and enhance customer experiences. Amazon's voice assistant, Alexa, is another example of how AI is integrated into its product offerings.
2. **Tesla:** Tesla has revolutionized the automotive industry by integrating AI into its vehicles. The company's self-driving technology, powered by

AI, is continuously learning from road data, improving the safety and efficiency of autonomous driving. Tesla's use of AI extends to its manufacturing process, where AI-driven robots and systems enhance production efficiency.

3. **Google:** Google leverages AI in nearly every aspect of its business, from search engine algorithms to personalized ad targeting. The company's AI research division, Google Brain, has made groundbreaking advancements in machine learning, including the development of TensorFlow, an

open-source platform used by developers worldwide to create AI applications.

These case studies highlight how AI is not just a tool but a central component in driving innovation and growth for modern businesses.

Section 5: Ethics and Risks of AI

Ethics in AI: Key Questions

As Artificial Intelligence becomes more advanced and embedded in society, ethical considerations have taken center stage. One of the primary ethical concerns is whether AI can operate without bias. Since AI systems are trained on data created by humans, there is always the potential for inherent biases to be reflected in the AI's decision-making processes. These biases can influence everything from hiring practices to criminal justice systems, potentially leading to unfair or harmful outcomes.

Another ethical issue is accountability. Who is responsible when an AI system makes a mistake, especially when it involves critical decisions like medical diagnoses or autonomous driving? With human oversight often limited, the line of responsibility can become blurred, raising complex legal and ethical questions.

Furthermore, ethical concerns arise over the autonomy of AI. As AI systems gain more decision-making power, there are fears that humans may lose control over the very systems they create. This leads to debates about the moral rights of AI—should advanced AI systems be treated with the same ethical considerations as humans or remain as tools under human control?

Privacy and Security Concerns

AI's ability to collect, analyze, and process vast amounts of data presents a significant privacy risk. With the rise of AI-powered surveillance systems, personal data can be collected without individuals' knowledge or consent. This has sparked concerns about data privacy, especially in industries like healthcare, finance, and social media, where sensitive information is at risk.

AI-powered facial recognition systems, for example, can track people in public spaces, raising concerns about mass surveillance and the erosion of individual privacy. The misuse of such technologies could lead to violations of personal freedoms and human rights.

Security is another major issue. As AI systems become more integrated into critical infrastructures like energy grids, healthcare, and transportation, they also become potential targets for cyberattacks. Hackers could exploit vulnerabilities in AI algorithms, leading to catastrophic consequences. Ensuring the safety and integrity of AI systems will be a major challenge as the technology continues to evolve.

The Impact of AI on the Job Market

One of the most hotly debated topics in AI ethics is its impact on the job market. AI and automation are poised to revolutionize industries, with machines replacing many tasks traditionally performed by humans. Jobs in manufacturing, customer service, and even some sectors of healthcare and finance are already being affected by AI-driven automation.

While AI will create new jobs, the concern is that the speed at which AI is advancing could outpace workers' ability to adapt. Low-skill jobs are most at risk, but even high-skill positions are not immune. The shift toward an AI-driven economy may exacerbate inequality if workers are not reskilled and prepared for the new job market.

Governments and businesses need to work together to ensure that workers displaced by AI have access to training and education programs that allow them to transition into new roles. The future of work will depend heavily on how societies manage the transition to an AI-dominated workforce.

Can AI Become a Threat to Humanity?

The question of whether AI could pose an existential threat to humanity is a subject of ongoing debate. Some experts, like Stephen Hawking and Elon Musk, have warned of the potential dangers of superintelligent AI—an AI that surpasses human intelligence and gains the ability to make decisions independently of human input. If such an AI were to prioritize its own goals over human values, it could lead to catastrophic outcomes.

While current AI systems are far from reaching that level of intelligence, the rapid pace of technological development raises concerns about future scenarios where AI systems might act unpredictably or beyond human control. This has led to calls for stronger safeguards and ethical frameworks to ensure that AI development remains aligned with human values and safety.

AI Regulation and Policy

As AI technology advances, there is a growing need for regulations and policies to ensure that it is used responsibly. Governments around the world are beginning to recognize the importance of establishing clear rules for AI development and deployment. Regulations must address ethical concerns, privacy, security, and the impact of AI on society.

One of the main challenges in regulating AI is finding the right balance between fostering innovation and ensuring safety. Overly restrictive regulations could stifle technological progress, while lax regulations could lead to misuse or harmful outcomes. Policymakers must work closely with industry leaders, researchers, and ethicists to create frameworks that promote safe, transparent, and accountable AI.

International cooperation will also be crucial, as AI is a global technology. Standards for AI ethics, transparency, and security should be established across borders to prevent the misuse of AI technologies and ensure that they are used for the benefit of all.

Section 6: AI and the Future of Technology

AI in the Future: Predictions

The future of Artificial Intelligence holds endless possibilities, with predictions that AI will not only continue to enhance current technologies but also give rise to entirely new industries. AI's integration with other cutting-edge technologies, such as quantum computing and the Internet of Things (IoT), is expected to unlock unprecedented advancements in various fields.

One major prediction is that AI will become increasingly human-like in its ability to understand emotions, intent, and context. Advances in natural language processing and emotional AI could lead to machines that are capable of interacting with humans in a much more intuitive and personalized manner. This could revolutionize industries like customer service, healthcare, and entertainment, where human-machine interaction is key.

AI is also predicted to play a central role in solving some of humanity's biggest challenges, such as climate change, disease outbreaks, and global poverty. AI-powered models will help scientists better understand complex systems, make more accurate predictions, and develop innovative solutions.

AI-Driven Technologies (Robots, Autonomous Vehicles)

Robotics and autonomous vehicles are two areas where AI is expected to drive major technological breakthroughs. In robotics, AI is enabling machines to perform tasks with increasing autonomy and precision. Robots are already being used in factories, healthcare settings, and even homes to perform repetitive or dangerous tasks. As AI continues to advance, we can expect robots to become more intelligent and capable of complex problem-solving.

Autonomous vehicles, including self-driving cars, trucks, and drones, represent one of the most promising applications of AI. Companies like Tesla, Waymo, and Uber are at the forefront of developing AI-powered vehicles that can navigate roads, avoid obstacles, and make decisions in real-time. In the future, fully autonomous transportation systems could reduce traffic accidents, improve fuel efficiency, and revolutionize logistics.

AI will also drive the development of smart cities, where autonomous vehicles and robots seamlessly interact with public infrastructure to optimize traffic flow, manage resources, and improve the quality of urban life.

How AI is Changing the Internet and Social Media

The Internet and social media are already heavily influenced by AI, and this influence is only expected to grow. AI algorithms are behind the personalized feeds on platforms like Facebook, Twitter, and Instagram, determining what content users see based on their preferences and behavior. In the future, AI could take personalization to new levels, curating even more tailored experiences for users.

AI is also changing the way content is created and consumed online. For example, AI-powered tools can now generate text, images, and even videos with minimal human input. Deepfake technology, which uses AI to create realistic but entirely fabricated content, presents both opportunities and risks for the future of media and communication.

As AI continues to shape the digital landscape, concerns about data privacy, misinformation, and online manipulation will need to be addressed. Ensuring that

AI systems operate transparently and ethically will be essential to maintaining trust in digital platforms.

The Future of AI in Education

AI is poised to transform education, making learning more personalized, accessible, and efficient. In the future, AI-driven systems will offer even more advanced forms of adaptive learning, providing students with real-time feedback and tailored content that matches their individual learning styles. This could lead to improved outcomes and a more inclusive educational experience.

Virtual classrooms powered by AI will allow students from around the world to access high-quality education, regardless of their location. AI will also play a key role in teacher support, automating administrative tasks and providing insights into student performance, enabling educators to focus on what matters most—teaching.

In the long term, AI could help redefine the role of education itself, shifting the focus from rote memorization to critical thinking, creativity, and problem-solving. As the job market evolves with AI, lifelong learning will become essential, and AI will likely be central to helping individuals continuously reskill and upskill throughout their careers.

AI Predictions for the Next Decade

Looking ahead, the next decade is expected to bring unprecedented advancements in AI. Some key predictions include:

- **General AI:** While still a distant goal, researchers are making strides toward creating AI that can perform a wide range of tasks, much like a human. If achieved, this could radically alter the nature of work, society, and human-computer interaction.

- **AI in Healthcare:** AI will play a pivotal role in personalized medicine, predictive healthcare, and the development of new treatments. AI-driven diagnostics and virtual health assistants will become commonplace, improving healthcare accessibility and outcomes.
- **Sustainability and Climate Change:** AI will help optimize energy use, monitor environmental changes, and develop solutions to combat climate change. AI-powered models will assist in better resource management and more efficient production processes.

- **AI and Ethics:** As AI grows more powerful, ethical considerations will take center stage. The development of robust AI governance frameworks will be critical to ensuring that AI is used for the benefit of humanity, rather than to its detriment.

The future of AI is filled with potential, but it also brings with it significant challenges that must be addressed thoughtfully and collaboratively. The decisions we make today will shape the trajectory of AI in the decades to come.

Section 7: How to Get Started with AI

Key Steps for AI Beginners

Getting started with Artificial Intelligence might seem daunting, but it becomes manageable if approached methodically. The first key step is understanding the fundamentals of AI, machine learning, and data science. Beginners should start by familiarizing themselves with the core concepts of AI, such as algorithms, neural networks, and data processing. A basic understanding of mathematics, particularly linear algebra, statistics, and calculus, is essential to grasp how AI systems work.

Once you've gained theoretical knowledge, the next step is to start coding. Most beginners begin with simple programming exercises to understand how algorithms are implemented in code. At this stage, selecting the right tools and platforms for AI development is crucial, as they will allow you to experiment and practice building AI models.

Choosing the Right Programming Language for AI

Choosing the right programming language for AI is an important decision that can affect your learning curve and productivity. Python is widely considered the best programming language for AI due to its simplicity, vast libraries, and strong community support. Libraries such as TensorFlow, PyTorch, and Scikit-learn provide pre-built tools to simplify the AI development process.

Other languages like R, Julia, and Java are also used in AI projects, depending on specific needs. R is popular for statistical analysis, while Java is used in large-scale enterprise AI solutions. However, Python remains the go-to choice for most AI learners and professionals.

Best Resources for Learning AI

There is a wealth of resources available for those interested in learning AI. Online platforms such as Coursera, edX, and Udacity offer comprehensive AI courses taught by leading universities and companies. Books like *"Artificial Intelligence: A Modern Approach"* by Stuart Russell and Peter Norvig are highly recommended for foundational knowledge.

For hands-on learning, websites like Kaggle provide datasets and competitions that allow beginners to practice building AI models. Additionally, AI-related blogs, podcasts, and YouTube channels offer valuable insights and keep you updated on the latest trends and advancements in AI.

Practical AI Project Examples

To truly understand AI, it's important to work on practical projects that apply the concepts you've learned. Beginners can start with small-scale projects, such as:

- **Image Classification:** Building an AI model that can recognize and categorize images.
- **Chatbot Development:** Creating a simple AI chatbot that responds to user queries.
- **Predictive Analytics:** Using AI to predict trends based on historical

data (e.g., stock market trends, weather forecasting).

Working on these projects will help you gain experience in coding, model training, and problem-solving with AI.

Building Your First AI Project

Your first AI project is a significant milestone, and it's important to select a project that is challenging yet manageable. Start by defining a clear goal, such as predicting house prices using a dataset or creating an AI model that identifies objects in images. Break the project into smaller tasks—data collection, data cleaning, model selection, training, and testing.

Once the project is complete, evaluate your model's performance and identify areas for improvement. Sharing your project on platforms like GitHub and engaging with the AI community will help you receive feedback and continue refining your skills.

Section 8: Machine Learning in Detail

What is Machine Learning?

Machine Learning (ML) is a subset of AI that focuses on building systems capable of learning from data and improving their performance over time without explicit programming. In essence, machine learning enables computers to recognize patterns and make decisions based on data inputs, allowing them to "learn" from experience.

ML is divided into three main types: **Supervised Learning**, where models are trained on labeled data; **Unsupervised Learning**, where models learn from unlabeled data to find hidden patterns; and **Reinforcement Learning**, where models learn by receiving rewards or penalties based on their actions.

Key Machine Learning Algorithms

There are several machine learning algorithms, each suited to different types of problems. Some of the most commonly used algorithms include:

- **Linear Regression:** Used for predicting continuous values based on input variables.
- **Decision Trees:** Used for classification and regression tasks by splitting data into decision nodes.
- **K-Nearest Neighbors (KNN):** A simple algorithm that classifies data

points based on their proximity to other data points.

- **Support Vector Machines (SVM):** A powerful algorithm used for classification by finding the optimal boundary between classes.
- **Random Forest:** An ensemble method that creates multiple decision trees to improve accuracy and reduce overfitting.

Each of these algorithms has its strengths and is chosen based on the specific task and dataset at hand.

Neural Networks and How They Learn

Neural networks, inspired by the structure of the human brain, are a cornerstone of deep learning. These networks consist of layers of neurons (nodes) connected by weighted edges. When input data passes through the network, it is transformed at each layer based on the weights and activation functions, allowing the network to learn complex patterns.

The learning process in neural networks occurs through **backpropagation**, where errors are propagated backward through the network to adjust the weights, improving the model's performance over time. Neural networks are particularly effective for tasks such as image recognition, natural language processing, and game playing.

How Data Trains AI Models

The process of training AI models revolves around feeding them vast amounts of data to help them learn patterns and make predictions. The quality of the data is crucial for the success of the model. Typically, the dataset is divided into three parts:

- **Training Data:** Used to train the model and adjust parameters.
- **Validation Data:** Used to tune the model and prevent overfitting.

- **Test Data:** Used to evaluate the model's final performance.

During training, the AI model adjusts its internal parameters (such as weights in neural networks) to minimize the error between its predictions and the actual outcomes. Over time, this leads to more accurate predictions on new, unseen data.

Machine Learning Project Examples

To better understand machine learning, here are some practical project ideas:

- **Spam Detection:** Build a model to classify emails as spam or non-spam.

- **Recommendation System:** Develop a recommendation system like those used by Netflix or Amazon, suggesting movies or products based on user preferences.
- **Sentiment Analysis:** Use natural language processing to analyze the sentiment of social media posts or product reviews.

These projects will give you a hands-on experience in applying machine learning algorithms and techniques to solve real-world problems.

Section 9: Deep Learning and Neural Networks

What is Deep Learning?

Deep learning is a subset of machine learning that involves algorithms inspired by the structure and function of the brain's neural networks. Unlike traditional machine learning, where models are often shallow and use structured data, deep learning models can process and learn from massive amounts of unstructured data like images, audio, and text. What makes deep learning stand out is its ability to learn high-level features directly from raw data, reducing the need for manual feature engineering.

At the core of deep learning are **artificial neural networks (ANNs)**, which are composed of layers of nodes (or neurons) connected to one another. Each node takes inputs, applies a mathematical operation, and passes the result to the next layer of nodes. The deeper the network (i.e., the more layers it has), the more complex the patterns it can learn.

Neural Network Architectures

There are various types of neural network architectures, each designed for specific types of tasks. The most common architectures include:

- **Feedforward Neural Networks (FNN):** These are the simplest form of neural networks where information moves in only one direction—from input to output. They are used in basic classification tasks.
- **Convolutional Neural Networks (CNN):** CNNs are widely used for image recognition and processing tasks. They have convolutional layers that automatically detect spatial patterns like edges, shapes, and textures in images.

- **Recurrent Neural Networks (RNN):** These networks are designed to work with sequential data like time series, audio, or text. RNNs can retain information from previous inputs using a memory-like mechanism, making them ideal for tasks like speech recognition and language translation.
- **Autoencoders:** A type of unsupervised learning model, autoencoders are used for tasks like data compression and denoising. They work by reducing data to a lower-dimensional representation and then reconstructing it.

- **Generative Adversarial Networks (GANs):** GANs consist of two networks—a generator and a discriminator—that compete against each other to create realistic-looking data. They are primarily used for generating synthetic images and videos.

How Convolutional Neural Networks Work

Convolutional Neural Networks (CNNs) have become a standard in tasks like image classification, object detection, and image segmentation. The core idea behind CNNs is the **convolution operation**, where small filters are applied to the input data (typically images) to extract important features like edges and textures.

CNNs are composed of several key layers:

- **Convolutional Layer:** This layer applies convolution filters to the input, creating a feature map. It reduces the number of parameters, making the model more efficient in processing large images.
- **Pooling Layer:** After the convolutional layer, pooling layers downsample the feature maps, reducing the spatial dimensions while retaining the most important

information. This helps the network become invariant to small translations in the input data.

- **Fully Connected Layer:** At the final stage of a CNN, fully connected layers take the high-level features extracted by previous layers and make predictions based on them. These layers work similarly to traditional neural networks.

CNNs have been highly successful in various applications, from facial recognition systems to medical image analysis.

Recurrent Neural Networks and Their Applications

Recurrent Neural Networks (RNNs) are specifically designed to handle sequential data. Unlike traditional neural networks, RNNs have a unique architecture that allows them to maintain a "memory" of previous inputs. This makes them ideal for tasks where the order of data matters, such as:

- **Language Modeling:** RNNs are used to predict the next word in a sentence, which is essential in applications like speech recognition, machine translation, and text generation.

- **Time Series Forecasting:** RNNs can analyze trends in financial or weather data to make future predictions based on past events.
- **Speech Recognition:** RNNs power systems like Google Voice and Siri, converting spoken language into text by analyzing the temporal structure of audio signals.

However, RNNs struggle with long-term dependencies, which is where **Long Short-Term Memory (LSTM)** and **Gated Recurrent Unit (GRU)** models come into play. These advanced architectures are capable of learning long-range relationships, making them suitable for more complex tasks.

Projects Using Deep Learning

Practical experience is crucial in understanding deep learning. Here are some examples of deep learning projects:

- **Image Recognition System:** Train a deep learning model to classify objects in an image (e.g., distinguishing between different types of animals).
- **Natural Language Processing (NLP) Model:** Develop an RNN or

LSTM to generate text, summarize articles, or translate languages.

- **Speech-to-Text Converter:** Build a system that converts spoken audio into text using deep learning techniques in combination with RNNs and LSTMs.
- **AI Art Generator:** Using a GAN, create an AI that can generate original art or transform existing images into different artistic styles.

Section 10: AI for Entrepreneurs and Startups

How AI Helps Startups Grow

Artificial Intelligence offers numerous opportunities for startups to scale quickly and innovate more efficiently. Startups that incorporate AI into their business models can automate labor-intensive processes, gain insights from vast amounts of data, and enhance customer experiences.

AI-driven startups can use algorithms to analyze market trends, optimize supply chains, and streamline product development. For example, AI-powered recommendation engines allow e-commerce startups to suggest products based on customer behavior, boosting sales and customer engagement.

Additionally, AI tools can help startups reduce costs by automating tasks like customer support (with chatbots), fraud detection, and content moderation, allowing them to operate with smaller teams.

Using AI to Improve Customer Experience

Customer experience is a crucial factor for startup success, and AI can significantly improve how businesses interact with their customers. Some AI-driven methods to enhance customer experience include:

- **Personalization:** AI algorithms analyze customer preferences and behaviors to offer tailored product or content recommendations. For instance, Netflix uses AI to recommend movies and shows, while Amazon uses it to suggest products.
- **Chatbots and Virtual Assistants:** AI-powered chatbots can provide instant support to customers, answering common questions or assisting with purchases. This allows

businesses to offer 24/7 customer service, improving user satisfaction.

- **Sentiment Analysis:** AI tools can analyze customer feedback and social media mentions to gauge public sentiment toward a brand or product, helping startups respond to customer needs proactively.

Building an AI Team

For startups looking to implement AI, assembling a skilled AI team is essential. Typically, an AI team consists of several key roles:

- **Data Scientists:** These professionals are responsible for collecting, processing, and analyzing data, which is the foundation of AI models. They work on creating predictive models, identifying trends, and implementing machine learning algorithms.

- **AI/ML Engineers:** AI engineers focus on developing, testing, and deploying AI solutions. They work on coding algorithms, building models, and optimizing AI systems for real-world applications.
- **AI Researchers:** AI researchers push the boundaries of AI technologies, developing new algorithms and architectures to solve

specific problems. They are often involved in more experimental, long-term projects.

- **Business Strategists:** A strategist ensures that AI projects align with the company's overall business goals. They identify areas where AI can add value and help create a roadmap for AI integration within the company.

Funding and Investment for AI Startups

Securing funding is a critical step for AI startups, as developing AI technologies can be capital-intensive. Entrepreneurs can explore several funding options:

- **Venture Capital (VC):** Many VCs are eager to invest in AI startups due to the technology's growth potential. Having a well-structured business plan and a proof-of-concept can attract VC firms.
- **Government Grants:** Some governments offer grants or tax incentives for startups working on innovative technologies like AI, particularly in fields such as healthcare, education, and sustainability.

- **Corporate Partnerships:** Partnering with larger companies can provide startups with the resources they need to scale, including funding, technical support, and market access.
- **Crowdfunding:** Platforms like Kickstarter and Indiegogo can be used to generate early-stage funding from the general public. While crowdfunding may not be enough to fully develop an AI project, it can help gauge market interest and raise initial capital.

Case Studies of Successful AI Startups

Many startups have leveraged AI to achieve remarkable success. Some notable examples include:

- **OpenAI:** Founded as a research lab, OpenAI has pushed the boundaries of AI capabilities with its GPT models, which are used in industries ranging from education to customer support.
- **UiPath:** This startup focuses on robotic process automation (RPA), helping businesses automate repetitive tasks through AI. UiPath has grown into a billion-dollar company by enabling companies to reduce operational costs.

- **Lemonade:** An AI-driven insurance company, Lemonade uses algorithms to process claims faster and more efficiently than traditional insurers, transforming the insurance industry.

By studying these cases, entrepreneurs can learn how to navigate the AI landscape and apply successful strategies to their own ventures.

Section 11: Implementing AI in Companies

Assessing Your Company's Readiness for AI

Before diving into AI implementation, it's crucial for companies to evaluate their readiness. This process involves assessing several key factors:

- **Data Infrastructure:** AI relies on data, so it's essential to ensure that your company has a strong data infrastructure in place. This includes having access to clean, organized, and relevant data sets.

- **Technical Expertise:** Implementing AI requires specialized skills, including data science, machine learning, and AI engineering. Companies should evaluate their internal talent and determine if they need to hire or train personnel.
- **Business Objectives:** AI should align with your company's business goals. Identify areas where AI can create the most value, such as improving efficiency, enhancing customer experience, or generating new revenue streams.
- **Budget and Resources:** AI projects can be costly, requiring investment

in technology, infrastructure, and talent. Companies need to assess whether they have the financial capacity to support AI initiatives.

Integrating AI into Business Processes

Once your company is ready for AI, the next step is integrating it into existing business processes. AI can be applied in numerous ways, including:

- **Automation:** AI can automate repetitive tasks, freeing up employees to focus on more strategic work. This can include automating customer service inquiries, processing data, or managing supply chains.

- **Predictive Analytics:** AI can analyze historical data to make predictions about future trends, helping companies optimize marketing campaigns, manage inventory, or forecast demand.
- **Customer Interaction:** AI-driven chatbots and virtual assistants can enhance customer service by providing instant, personalized responses, reducing wait times, and improving customer satisfaction.
- **Decision-Making:** AI systems can help leaders make more informed

decisions by providing data-driven insights, identifying trends, and offering recommendations based on complex data analysis.

Choosing the Right AI Solutions

Selecting the right AI solutions is a critical step in successful implementation. Companies must consider their specific needs and goals when evaluating AI technologies. Some factors to consider include:

- **Customization:** Does the AI solution allow for customization to fit your specific business needs? Off-the-shelf solutions may be quicker to implement, but custom solutions can offer more tailored results.

- **Scalability:** Will the AI solution scale with your business as it grows? Ensure that the technology can handle increasing amounts of data and larger projects over time.
- **Integration:** How easily can the AI solution integrate with your existing systems and workflows? Smooth integration is key to minimizing disruption and maximizing efficiency.
- **Vendor Support:** Look for AI vendors that offer strong customer support, training, and

documentation. Proper guidance from the vendor can greatly accelerate implementation and troubleshooting.

Training Employees to Work with AI

For AI implementation to be successful, employees must be equipped with the right skills. This includes both technical training and fostering a culture that embraces AI innovation. Steps to train employees include:

- **Workshops and Training Programs:** Provide AI training programs that teach employees how to use new AI tools, interpret data insights, and integrate AI into their day-to-day work.

- **Upskilling and Reskilling:** AI will change many job roles, so it's important to focus on upskilling employees to handle more complex tasks, while reskilling others for new roles created by AI.
- **Collaboration between Humans and AI:** Encourage a collaborative environment where employees understand AI as a tool to enhance their work, not as a replacement.

Case Studies of AI Implementation in Different Industries

Many industries are already seeing the transformative power of AI. Some examples include:

- **Healthcare:** AI is revolutionizing healthcare by improving diagnostics, personalizing treatment plans, and analyzing medical images with higher accuracy than humans.
- **Retail:** Retailers use AI for inventory management, personalized shopping experiences, and optimizing supply chain logistics.
- **Finance:** Financial institutions leverage AI for fraud detection, risk management, and algorithmic

trading to improve decision-making processes.
- **Manufacturing:** AI is automating production lines, enhancing quality control, and predicting equipment maintenance needs through predictive analytics.

Section 12: The Future of Artificial Intelligence and Its Role in Society

The Future of Human-Machine Interaction

As AI becomes more advanced, the interaction between humans and machines will evolve dramatically. Future AI systems will be more intuitive, allowing for natural communication through speech, gestures, and even emotions. Some developments to expect include:

- **AI Personal Assistants:** AI-driven assistants will become even more integrated into daily life, offering proactive assistance based on individual needs and preferences.
- **Brain-Computer Interfaces:** Research is advancing on interfaces that allow direct communication between the brain and machines.

This could lead to AI-powered devices that respond to thoughts or neurological signals.

- **Human-Robot Collaboration:** Robots equipped with AI will increasingly work alongside humans in various industries, improving safety, efficiency, and productivity.

How AI Will Transform Jobs

The impact of AI on the job market is a widely debated topic. While AI will automate some roles, it will also create new jobs and opportunities for growth. Some changes to expect include:

- **Automation of Repetitive Tasks:** Jobs involving routine, repetitive tasks are the most likely to be automated by AI. This includes roles in manufacturing, data entry, and customer support.
- **New AI-Driven Roles:** As AI technologies evolve, new job roles will emerge, including AI trainers, data scientists, and AI ethicists. These jobs will require specialized knowledge of AI systems and data analysis.
- **Reskilling and Upskilling:** To stay competitive in the AI-driven job market, workers will need to

continuously learn and adapt to new technologies. Governments, educational institutions, and businesses will play a critical role in providing retraining opportunities.

Ethics and Governance of AI in Society

As AI continues to advance, ethical concerns will play an increasingly central role in its development and deployment. Some key ethical issues include:

- **Bias and Fairness:** AI systems can inherit biases from the data they are trained on, leading to unfair treatment of certain groups. Ensuring fairness in AI requires transparency and accountability in data collection and algorithm design.

- **Privacy and Surveillance:** AI technologies, particularly in the field of surveillance, raise concerns about privacy and data security. Proper regulation is needed to prevent misuse and protect individual rights.
- **Autonomy and Control:** As AI systems become more autonomous, questions arise about who is responsible for their actions. Clear governance frameworks must be established to regulate AI's decision-making processes.

AI in Culture and the Arts

AI is increasingly making its way into the world of culture and the arts, with AI-powered systems creating music, literature, and visual art. The use of AI in creative fields raises several interesting questions:

- **AI as an Artist:** Can AI truly create art, or is it simply replicating patterns it has learned? While AI can generate paintings, music, or poems, some argue that true creativity still requires human input.
- **AI-Assisted Creation:** Many artists are using AI as a tool to enhance their work, collaborating with

machines to generate new ideas and push the boundaries of creativity.
- **Cultural Representation:** As AI becomes more prevalent in art and culture, there is a need to ensure diverse cultural representation in AI-generated content, avoiding the risk of promoting stereotypes or biases.

The Future of Humanity in the Age of AI

As AI becomes an integral part of society, it will shape the future of humanity in profound ways. Some key trends to consider include:

- **Human Enhancement:** AI-powered technologies like prosthetics, brain-computer interfaces, and personalized medicine will enhance human abilities, potentially leading to a future where humans and machines merge in new ways.
- **Global Inequality:** There is a risk that AI could exacerbate global inequality if access to AI technologies is limited to certain regions or economic classes. Ensuring equitable distribution of AI's benefits will be a major challenge.

- **AI and Human Purpose:** As AI takes over more tasks, there will be a need for humans to find new forms of purpose and fulfillment. This could lead to a redefinition of work, leisure, and creativity in the AI age.

www.ingramcontent.com/pod-product-compliance
Lightning Source LLC
Chambersburg PA
CBHW071059240526
45471CB00016B/2171